Unexpected Destiny

A Story of Albinism, Adoption, Cross-Cultural Living, and a Search for Identity

Pat Estes
with Suzanne Kamara

WESTBOW®
PRESS
A DIVISION OF THOMAS NELSON
& ZONDERVAN

WestBow Press books may be ordered through booksellers or by contacting:

WestBow Press
A Division of Thomas Nelson & Zondervan
1663 Liberty Drive
Bloomington, IN 47403
www.westbowpress.com
1 (866) 928-1240

ISBN: 978-1-4908-3768-0 (sc)
ISBN: 978-1-4908-3770-3 (hc)
ISBN: 978-1-4908-3769-7 (e)

Library of Congress Control Number: 2014908979

Printed in the United States of America.

WestBow Press rev. date: 06/09/2014

Contents

To the memory of Suzy's birthmother,
Sassa Yamie Kamara,
and to
Joseph Humaru Kamara:
You have the wonderful privilege
of being the firstborn son of the couple
whose story is partially told here.
May you ever seek the Lord
and His perfect ways.

Forward

Pat Estes is a deeply spiritual woman who routinely amazes me with her insights about Scripture. Not content merely to read God's Word, she digs in to study it, apprehend truth, and apply it to her life. She is constantly aware of God's presence and is quick to follow his leading. *Unexpected Destiny* is her testimony of God's guidance in the lives of her, her husband, Joe, and their adopted daughter, Suzanne.

Born in Sierra Leone, West Africa, Suzanne is affected by albinism, a deficiency of skin pigmentation, and the accompanying astigmatism. When Pat and Joe adopted Suzy at the age of five weeks and eventually relocated to the United States, she began a journey of self-discovery filled with anguish and confusion. Feeling neither African nor American, black nor white, Suzy faced jeers at school, self-doubts, and deep questions about the character of God.

Pat's sensitive eyewitness account as a mother, spiritual mentor, and seeker after wisdom leads us to the inevitable conclusion that God's grace is sufficient in all circumstances.

Heather Gemmen Wilson
award-winning author and international speaker

Acknowledgments

The writing of this story has been a twenty-nine-year process, for when it seemed to be the right time to actually formulate a book, the first job was to gather the letters and journal entries that had been written over those years. Organizing the thoughts into a cohesive whole has taken twenty months with input from my husband, Joe, Suzy, and her husband.

Many others have helped us. Friends have read parts of the manuscript and given their suggestions and affirmations. More intense editing was done by Kara Youree, Brittany Marcello, and Lindsay Leck whose suggestions and grammar corrections were invaluable. Cultural content was checked by David Musa and Radcliffe and Sylvia Jones. Finally Mary McNeil completed a professional edit.

My thanks go to the staff at Westbow Press for their excellent work in the publication of this story.

Yet the greatest input is from the Lord Jesus, who has led us every step of the way, working all things together for our good and for His praise. To Him be the glory!

Map created for this publication by Jim Pardew.

Trust in the LORD and do good;
Dwell in the land and cultivate faithfulness.
Delight yourself in the LORD; And He will give you the desires of your heart.
Commit your way to the LORD, Trust also in Him, and He will do it.
He will bring forth your righteousness as the light
And your judgment as the noonday.
Rest in the LORD and wait patiently for Him.
(Psalm 37:3–7)

Introduction

Unexpected destiny. My husband Joe and I never anticipated and could not have imagined the plans God had for us when we began our life together forty-five years ago. We never dreamed that we would live in Africa or adopt children from different cultures. Nor did we think we would move to the Midwest and live out our lives in Indiana. But God has led each step and shown us amazing miracles along the way. Suzy's story is also one of unexpected destiny, a life of challenges, but a chronicle of surprising events that begs to be told.

I met and dated Joe during high school while searching for God. By age nineteen, I had learned Psalm 37:4: "Delight yourself in the LORD; and He will give you the desires of your heart." Very slowly I began to comprehend: God planned that I (and everyone else, but this is my history) should learn to know Him through His Son Jesus. As my relationship with Him grew, I would begin to understand how to follow His path for my life. At the same time, Joe was searching for God. We began to study the Bible separately and together, learning at what often seemed a snail's pace, to delight in Him. It was much later that this concept was clearly, but simply, illustrated for me through a fictitious conversation.

In a novel by Deanne Gist set in the late 1800s, Esther was a thirty-year-old single woman who believed she was being offered her last chance at marriage. The intended groom was a lifelong friend, but one whose position as a pastor demanded alterations in Esther's lifestyle. She willingly planned to forego her own aspirations, thinking that only marriage could complete her. Then her father suggested that she put God first, even above marriage.

". . . for now, why not embrace Christ fully and with abandon? Then see how you feel about marriage."

"How? How do I *embrace* Christ?" she asked.

"You obey Him. Dwell on His Word. Do every single thing for His glory.

Talk to Him, praise Him, delight in His creation. . . . sing to Him. Make Him the love of your life."[1]

Delighting in God. Putting Him first. Making Him the true love of one's life. Although I was learning this delight, I couldn't discount my longings. My list began with a husband, a big family, and the opportunity to become a teacher.

A teaching job opened up right out of college, and Joe and I were married soon afterward. But time passed, and we weren't getting pregnant. Then we learned that we couldn't have children of our own, and Joe wasn't open to the idea of adoption at that time. I had no alternative but to keep searching for God's answers to my yearnings.

Finally, after seven years of crying out to God for a child, I came to a place of acceptance. We had given our lives to Him; He would order them as He saw fit and somehow keep His promise in the process.

During the eighth year of our marriage, we saw beautiful slides of Sierra Leone's land and people at an unscheduled Saturday night church service. Missionary Dr. Marilyn Birch mentioned the need for a director of a recording studio in that country. Friends who knew us well began to say, "That's a job for you, Joe."

From childhood Joe had a consuming interest in film and radio. Early each morning he would wait in the elementary school office to cajole teachers into showing films so he could run the projector. In high school he fed this interest by joining the film and stage crews and taking a radio-drama-production class. Through college and a stint in the army, radio became his avocation, while his degree in psychology and sociology yielded a social services job. After settling in Olean, New York, he worked after hours as music director and DJ for the local radio station.

Dr. Birch's message and the comments of our friends started us thinking and discussing the impractical notion of dropping everything to head to Africa. Joe was about to reach tenure in his job, and besides, we had taken charge of our church's youth group. We couldn't desert the teens. Finally we decided to send for information about the position.

Return mail brought not information, but forms to complete. Over the next four months, we not only submitted the initial forms, but actually completed the entire application process, including psychological testing, while thinking, "It can't hurt." Thus we were shocked when a letter arrived inviting us to church headquarters in Marion, Indiana, as "the final step in appointment to Sierra Leone."

It would be too tedious here to embark on our whole story of God's leading. Joe and I recognized God's guidance through different circumstances. For me, it came through an unsolicited response to my long-term questioning. As part of the interview process, the psychologist mused, "Hmm. You don't have children. It's ten times easier on the mission field without children." It was like a light going on! Was this God's reason for our infertility? Would we be better able to fulfill our ministry because we didn't have a family?

Circumstances fell into place, and seven months after our visit to Marion we were headed to a whole new way of life in Sierra Leone, West Africa. Shopping in the capital city of Freetown, viewing the countryside so different from our home area, and then traveling in the back of the lorry (a covered pick-up) half-full of groceries and suitcases for the last bouncing twenty miles of our journey, we finally reached the mission home awaiting us 137 miles "up-country." We were overwhelmed with unfamiliar sights, sounds and even smells. There were the challenges of continuous tropical heat, meeting and working with missionary colleagues, and learning about the beautiful and friendly African people.

As director of the recording studio, Joe soon learned his work: producing radio programs in seven languages for pastors, for the mission radio station (ELWA) in Monrovia, Liberia, and later for the Sierra Leone government station. This could only be accomplished with an African assistant, Abdulai Sheriff, who had previously worked at the studio, knew the dialects, and could edit the programs. Abdulai also gave cultural help and advice. In the dry season, studio teams would show gospel films in villages in the open air.

God was answering our deeply felt, unconscious requests in ways we never expected. Joe was back at work in film and radio, and I soon had the opportunity to teach in children's services and in the local Bible school.

It was not until the month of Suzanne's birth, eight more years later, that I read these words from *Beyond the Wall* by Hank Paulson:

> God . . . had already set a new compass-bearing for my life, one that would direct me irresistibly toward [His] calling. And, being God, He didn't even trouble to consult me beforehand! I guess I should have known when I committed my destiny into His hands years earlier that I was leaving myself open

> to the "risk" that He would come up with something unthinkable. Something I would never have predicted. . . . Something so surprisingly "right" for me that once I was into it, I would quickly find it impossible to imagine myself doing anything else with satisfaction![2]

Mr. Paulson's "calling" was very different from our own, but his words hit the mark. We had left ourselves open to "something unthinkable. Something [we] never would have predicted" by agreeing to go to Africa in the first place. Little did we realize how satisfaction would come through that life-changing decision.

After Suzanne's arrival, I reread Mr. Paulson's words. Once again God had come up with "something [we] would never have predicted," and, yes, it was "surprisingly 'right.'" We could no longer imagine life without her.

Our hearts' desires have been satisfied in many ways through the years, in the gifts of Suzanne and her brother Peter, and much later through their spouses and our grandchildren. Beyond this, God has led us and taught us to trust Him. He will continue to order our lives through the unimaginable, unexpected destiny He has in store.

1

Turning Point

"I'm not African! I'm not American! I'm not black, and I'm not white!" blasted fourteen-year-old Suzanne, baring the pain in her heart. She knew she was African, born in Sierra Leone of African parents. She also knew she was an American citizen. If she couldn't remember our visit to the Indianapolis courthouse for naturalization when she was five, she was familiar with the pictures. Still, this anguish had defined her confusion and shaped her life. For as long as she could remember, she had struggled to discover where she fit, stating her anger at God that she looked "different."

What about Suzanne has elicited stares from strangers and cutting remarks from classmates? She has albinism, and her blonde hair and peach-colored skin with African features don't match up for those who want everyone placed neatly into a box of their own defining. Time would prove that she has perfect skin; hers is a partial albinism. Yet she is troubled by the severe astigmatism and mild nystagmus (eye shaking) that normally accompanies this condition. Her appearance was not like most of her peers, and they didn't seem to mind pointing it out or questioning her heritage.

Suzanne's confusion grew until it reached a climax in her early teens. Something had to be done to help our daughter.

The Beginning of the Promise

Delight yourself in the LORD;
And He will give you the desires of your heart.
—Psalm 37:4

2

The Shooting Star

Nine-year-old Ansu Kamara had never seen a shooting star like this one with the accompanying sound like the popping of fireworks. What could it mean?

Ansu and his friends were playing tag near their homes in Bafodia, Sierra Leone, on that February night. Their bare feet stirred the dry, powdery ground as they skittered across the irregular quadrangle at the center of the village. The Harmattan wind that had tirelessly blown chilled air from the Sahara since late December also brought tiny bits of sand that settled on every inanimate object. As the sun slipped behind the hills, the wind eased and the sky cleared somewhat. Odors from surrounding cooking fires had mostly faded; some neighbors were just completing their evening meal of cassava or potato leaves cooked with palm oil and meat or fish spooned over the staple rice.

There was no thought of the date or that this night was anything special until the boys saw the shooting star.

"I wonder what important person has died," whispered Ansu's friend. "Or what important person has been born."

Ansu's grandmother, the village midwife, and his mother, best friend of Sassa Yamie Kamara*, were at her home that night to help with the birth of Sassa's twins. However, Sassa died soon after her tiny babies were born prematurely, a light-skinned blond girl born first and only slightly larger than her darker-skinned brother. Larry and Cindy Marshall, resident missionaries of the village, offered to help care for the babies until a plan could be made for them, and the family agreed. They wanted them kept safe and in a good environment.

Twenty years later, Ansu would be reminded of that night, the shooting star, and the tiny, motherless twins.

*Sharing the same last name did not make Ansu and Sassa close relatives. The name Kamara is as common in their village as Smith or Jones is to Americans.

Bafodia village

Bafodia seen from the mission house on the hill

3

April Fools

It was April 1, 1985, but April Fools' jokes held no meaning in the African culture. Friends were coming to our village of Gbendembu (ben-*dem*-bu) for the annual weeklong Women's Institute, a retreat for women from churches across Sierra Leone.

Cindy Marshall brought the attendees from Bafodia. After dropping them off at their quarters, she eased her blue Mazda truck down our long, rocky driveway. I walked out to meet her but was astounded when she handed me an infant, now five weeks old but newborn-sized. She asked, "Will you take her?" Was this an April Fools' joke? Cindy later told me she meant "Will you hold her for me?" But I responded, "I would love to take her!" After all the years of dreaming Joe and I could have children, I was thrilled at the possibility that this child could be ours.

Cindy related the story of the twins born February 22, which happened to be my sixteenth wedding anniversary with Joe. When the babies' mother died soon after giving birth, Cindy and her husband, Larry, offered to temporarily care for them. The Marshalls held the twins close to warm them with their own bodies. Yet, in spite of their efforts, the little boy only survived until morning. With good care and a strong will (as we would later learn), plus God's hand on her life, the baby girl survived and even began to thrive. Soon a family representative brought an announcement to Cindy and Larry: "We're giving you this child."

Joe later realized he had met the twins' birthmother. We were in Bafodia earlier that February for a film campaign, and a woman, large with the twins she carried, had walked up the long hill to the mission house seeking assistance. Joe was outside taking pictures of fires that were set to burn off the remains of the recent harvest, and she asked him to snap her photograph. Then to his surprise, she entreated, "Please, take my babies," perhaps sensing that she would not survive their birth. Joe responded, "I'll just take one." How prophetic were those words!

Years later, Suzanne wondered how her family could say they loved her and yet seemingly abandon her. Without available medical help or extra money for milk, and because of Suzanne's diminutive size (less than four pounds at birth), it would have been very difficult for anyone in the village to take over her care. Added to this was the fact of high infant mortality in Sierra Leone, even for average-sized, healthy babies. But the missionaries would have the resources to provide for her needs; maybe she would have a chance of survival.

Painting by Suzy's Aunt Joy D'Angelo, representing Sassa and her premature twins.

Larry and Cindy seriously considered adopting Ginger (so named for her reddish-blonde hair), but Cindy's thinking changed while reading a children's book, *Little Lost Angel*[3] to four-year-old Jordan. In the story, a cherub who came with other heavenly messengers to announce the birth of Jesus was left behind. While searching for the way back to heaven, she was drawn to a light and was welcomed to the home of a couple who had long wished for children. They happily raised her as their own daughter. Through this simple story, Cindy came to believe that God's plan for Ginger involved a childless couple. Options were considered, especially among African pastors, but nothing worked out until she came to our home.

With a house full of visitors, I slipped out behind the building that housed our noisy generator to pour out my heart to God. His promise remained, "He will give you the desires of your heart" (Psalm 37:4). Yet the hope that Ginger could be our daughter warred with the equal possibility that she would never be ours.

I shared my feelings with Joe that night. He needed time to process this new idea and spent three long days thinking and praying about details that would follow adoption: immigration to the United States, family reaction, schooling, insurance, and many others. Then a question presented itself to him: "Well, Joe, do you want to be a father? This is your opportunity." He did want the chance to parent this precious baby.

Christian author Catherine Marshall once asked, "At moments when the future is completely obscured ... can any one of us afford to meet our tomorrows with dragging feet? God had been in the past. Then He would be in the future, too."[4] No, we would not drag our feet, but trust God with our future and that of Ginger.

Once the decision was made to adopt, we contacted Larry by ham radio and he gave his blessing for Ginger to join our family. We then took many pictures to send to our families. Her beauty would win the day and their approval.

Gifts came from African friends, missionaries, and visitors from the States and her needs were met. When Joe finally held her, he said, "Her name should be Suzanne." Then a friend suggested the middle name Renee. How appropriate: Suzanne Renee, "a lily reborn."

With no phone and only snail mail, the first message we received in response was a telegram from Joe's dad. "Overjoyed with the news," he wrote. "How Great Thou Art! Pray all goes well." The message surprised us, as Dad usually didn't speak of God or prayer. We knew he was excited about the prospect of a new grandchild. Later, letters from both of our mothers confirmed their joy in welcoming this new little one into the family.

4

A Mother's Wish

"I have heard and understand the adoption papers," asserted Suzanne's uncle, meeting with our lawyer and us in the capital city of Freetown. "But I can't sign them. Our family wants to see the child every two to five years so we can know firsthand of her welfare."

It was September 1985. Suzanne had lived in our home and hearts for five months. Her uncle's wish wasn't feasible, especially after we would return to the States. What would we do if the papers weren't signed, the first step toward a visa and US adoption?

The lawyer calmly responded, "There are no conditions in this process. The adopting family is responsible for the care and education of the child. You have to decide what you are going to do."

"I can't sign," repeated her uncle.

In a seemingly hopeless situation, we turned to God. He had already worked miracles in Suzanne's young life; we could trust Him with this new challenge.

The answer came quickly. As light was dawning the next morning, Suzanne's uncle knocked at our door.

"I'm signing the papers," he declared. "The mother has spoken and will bring trouble if I don't obey. Last night the child's mother came to me in a dream, carrying her baby boy on her back. She told me, 'I have one child with me and the other I see every day. I like what's happening with my child, and I don't want you to bother those people.'"

Suzy's family, among other Sierra Leoneans, is persuaded that ancestors can still affect their lives. They also believe that dreams have great significance. These strong convictions brought an urgency to settle the matter quickly.

Our next step seemed as insurmountable as the first. We needed the signature on adoption papers of Suzanne's grandfather, Alimamy Salifu Mansaray, the paramount chief in her village of Bafodia, witnessed by the district officer from Kabala. In this mountainous region it was an arduous trip between these villages even in the best of times. Sections of the singular unpaved road flaunted rocky heaps of crevices and mounds to be navigated by our four-cylinder Mazda pickup. Additionally, our home was four hours in another direction down the main road to Freetown. Again we prayed. Then, during a daily shortwave radio contact that October, friends at the missionary kids' school in Kabala broke in to say, "We hear that the district officer is going to Bafodia tomorrow. You might want to meet him there."

We hurriedly packed and started out, spending the night with friends in Kabala. We continued our journey around noon the next day. The hot sun and humid conditions combined to make dust stick to our perspiration-soaked clothes while we traversed the uneven road. Finally we reached the hill leading to the Bafodia mission house on the way into the village. Larry and Cindy welcomed us with cold drinks before we headed to the chief's compound.

Many gathered to see the strangers and to witness the event that was taking place. Suzanne's family members were happy to see her but eager to complete the adoption. They had heard of the dream and were anxious to comply with her deceased mother's wishes, as her uncle had been. The chief and district officer were also amenable. How grateful we felt as we witnessed their thumbprint signatures being added to the documents.

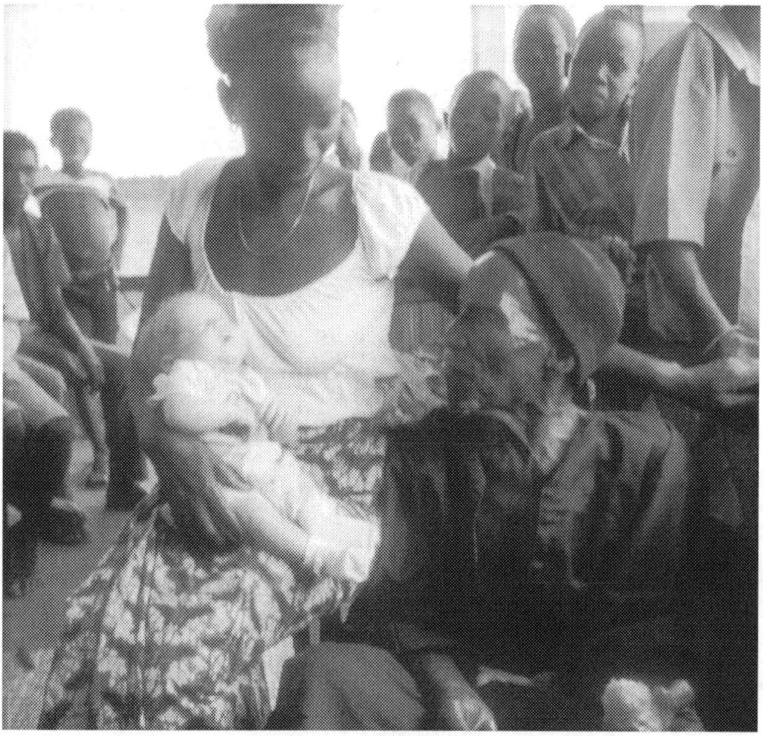

Suzanne meets her grandfather, paramount chief Alimamy Salifu Mansaray

5

Celebration

The adoption was finally registered with the Sierra Leone government, and it was time to celebrate. We scheduled a vacation by the ocean with our baby girl, staying in the beach house of another mission organization. We enjoyed basking in warm breezes on the semiprivate beach facing the Atlantic Ocean. It was a great setting for real relaxation. My joy was expressed in a poem:

I ran with you on the beach today,
You squealed with delight holding on tight.
We sat together at the shoreline
You, Daddy, and I,
Waiting for the water to tickle our feet.

Daddy dug a pool for you
And again . . . and again
When the water swept it full of sand.
Over and over you lifted your hand to your lips
For a mouthful of sand.

When I wiped your hand and face,
The other sandy thumb took its place.

You reached out for the waves
Then splashed in your pool
Until salt water was in your eyes.
You didn't cry—
You were reveling (even as we were),
In the glory of wind, waves, and sand.

We have two weeks to enjoy the beach.
We'll come back tomorrow
To play in the waves.
It's twice as much fun with you.

At the end of December, Suzanne was dedicated to God in our village church by our pastor and friend, Rev. Philip Sesay. We observed the occasion with a party in our backyard. Friends killed a sheep and cooked the specialty Jollof rice, an enticing meal of chicken and, in this case, lamb, cooked with parboiled rice and select spices, in a tomato-based sauce and ever-present hot pepper to taste. There were also sweet potatoes, thick peanut-butter "soup" over white rice, thinly peeled oranges to squeeze and suck the juice (only the sheep or goats would eat the membranes of an orange), cake and soft drinks for approximately seventy friends from our village and a few missionaries who attended. Joe told Suzanne's story, and Scripture was read. There was joyful singing and games for the children. Either from excitement or exhaustion, Suzanne slept through most of the festivities! It was truly a celebration of the unexpected destiny we were experiencing with our precious child.

Suzanne and her adoptive parents, Joe and Pat Estes

6

"Let's Go!"

One of Suzanne's early words was *go* as we continued the work of the studio. During the rainy season (May–November), we recorded sermons by pastors in their native languages to be edited by our African assistant. When the dry season came (December–April) studio teams visited villages with gospel films, hanging a canvas screen and using a generator for light and electricity. Local pastors translated the films, and people walked from distant villages, sometimes over many miles, to view Bible stories displayed on a screen. The hearts of many were opened to know God and His Son, Jesus.

A film campaign was scheduled for February in Bafodia, as it had been the year before, and we were there for Suzanne's first birthday. Family members enjoyed seeing her again and brought gifts of rice, bananas, peanuts, and live chickens. We met her birthfather, Saiyo Mansaray, and took his picture holding Suzanne. Friends came for a small party of lunch and cake.

Soon we were ready to "go" on a longer journey. By September 1986 we had obtained Suzanne's Sierra Leone passport and visitor's visa. We were on our way to the States for a three-month furlough.

This was an opportunity to reconnect with family and friends who supported us. Many were anxious to see the baby they had heard about and prayed for, and she was warmly welcomed by both of our families.

Three months were extended to six when our church headquarters asked Joe to take charge of audiovisuals for the missions department. He began this role, but we soon had to return to Sierra Leone for a permanent visa and to transfer the recording work to our African assistant. We were back in our village of Gbendembu from March to May of 1987.

When our friend Philip learned we would relocate to Indiana in a short time, he commented, "I understand the church has asked you to move, but what do you feel?"

"We have loved ones here and in the States," Joe responded. "It's difficult for us to think of leaving permanently."

"Then I am satisfied," concluded Philip. He, his wife, Sallay, and their family have remained good friends all through the years.

One memorable night during Holy Week, Suzanne was holding my hand as we walked across the mission compound under starry skies. I was feeling incredibly grateful for her and was expressing my thanks to God.

She was also "talking" softly in her baby language. Our spirits seemed in touch with each other and our Father. It was a very special moment.

Joe applied for Suzanne's permanent visa at the American Embassy in Freetown, learning that approval was needed through an office in Rome, Italy! Much later we heard from Paul Lawrence, a former co-worker of Joe's in Social Services, that he had gathered our documents and petitioned the State of New York for a pre-adoption certificate. The office in Rome was then contacted and the news came back to us that Suzanne had been classified as "the immediate relative of an American citizen." This gave us the right to formally request her immigrant's visa. Later Paul apologized for "butting into our business." On the contrary, his help was invaluable. By the end of May the three of us were on our way to America once again.

Challenges and Adjustments

Commit your way to the LORD;
Trust also in Him, and He will do it.
—Psalm 37:5

7

Peter Joseph

"There will be more children," I remarked to Joe after Suzanne's arrival. "Suzanne will need a sibling." He was not so sure. Praying for this seemed like ingratitude. We could no longer doubt that God was absolutely in control of planning our family. He would continue to guide us.

By the time we settled in an Indianapolis apartment, we were ready to pursue a second adoption through a local Christian agency. Dialogue with a caseworker that began in September led to the submission of our applications and autobiographies by March of 1988.

The caseworker seemed eager to complete the process, implementing three home studies within just a few weeks. She already had someone in mind for us but was careful not to give information prematurely.

I asked, "Does this mean we could have a 'placement' within the next couple of months?"

"Yes," was all she could reveal.

Suzanne was very excited at the prospect of a new baby. She wanted a brother, and we knelt together to present her request to God. At the end of May, we all attended a local hospital class, "Room for One More." A video presented thoughts and feelings older siblings sometimes have when a new baby arrives. Suzanne had the chance to diaper a doll and visit the nursery, but she cried as we walked away from viewing the babies. Did she think we would be taking one home with us?

She didn't have long to wait. A phone call from our caseworker just four days later carried the message, "I have a boy to talk with you about." It was a whirlwind day. Joe came home from work, we left Suzanne with a neighbor, and hurried to see pictures and learn information about this baby boy. He was classified as biracial, of black American and Italian heritage, and therefore listed as special needs. Really? I could not comprehend this classification.

We were surprised to learn that he was born on February 23, the day after Suzanne's birthday, exactly three years after she lost her twin brother in Bafodia.

Our caseworker suggested we take some time to decide, but this also confused me. I couldn't fathom saying, "No, we don't care for this one. We'll wait to see if a better one comes along," as if we were choosing a new piece of furniture. We had prayed for months for this child. Of course we wanted him and asked when we could have him. "Give me an hour," she replied.

Picking up Suzanne (and a check), we returned to meet our precious three-month-old baby who had been in the care of a foster mother since a few days after his birth.

The flat rate for an adoption at that time was $6500. "But," we were told, "in special circumstances the cost can be reduced to $3500, and I believe your case qualifies." For one thing, our first adoptee was a well-adjusted, happy three-year-old. Perhaps another reason was Peter's ethnicity, considering Suzanne's African heritage. Joe soon remembered a savings account he had opened ten years earlier. Its current balance of $3600 would cover the cost with just a little extra. God had led us to prepare for this expenditure long before we ever thought to move toward adoption.

As we completed the necessary documents, we were surprised to be asked, "What's his name going to be?" Yet there was no question; only the night before we had talked about a boy's name. "Peter Joseph," Joe said without hesitation, after his own grandfather and his great-uncle Peter.

It felt strange to be leaving the office with baby Peter. We were "shell-shocked"; so much had changed in just a few hours. Three-year-old Suzanne announced, "We're going to McDonald's!" No problem; we couldn't even think. While Joe and Suzanne finished their meal, I made a quick trip to the department store across the street for diapers and formula before we headed to church. Our son was introduced to new friends and his first Wednesday evening service.

For me, the adjustment to a second baby seemed greater than we had previously experienced, as sudden and unexpected as Suzanne's arrival had been. There were more complicated emotions to deal with, even just among our family of four. Early on the day after we brought Peter home, Suzanne was asking, "Where's *his* mother?" Slowly we all settled in to enjoying our new relationships.

Just after Peter's second birthday and Suzanne's fifth, we bought a home in Indianapolis, where we have lived ever since. Suzanne was loved by many friends, but especially by her little brother. Peter patiently allowed her to "run the show." They often played church. Suzanne was the preacher and Peter the song leader and congregation. He was the "pesky brother" at times, but he became her biggest defender and one who always loved her.

Suzanne and her brother, Peter

8

School Days

Suzanne happily climbed up the big steps of the school bus headed for the local public kindergarten with excitement for learning and adventure, while Peter ran down the street after the bus, crying, "I'm five. I can go to school!" Suzy loved school and the interaction with other children. At parent orientation her teacher commented, "Suzanne is doing well, and she will go far with her loving, caring attitude toward others."

We arranged to carpool with two neighborhood families and their daughters for the trip home after half-day sessions. Even with our outreach to these families, the other two girls quickly became fast friends, and Suzanne was the uninvited third wheel. She began to feel the need for a close neighborhood friend of her own.

Things had changed for Suzanne almost from the first day of school. She was "different," and her classmates and, even more, her bus-mates seemed bent on letting her know it. She was a happy and creative child at home or with close friends but began to be anxious and worried at school and in other public places. The thick glasses needed to correct her albino astigmatism added fuel to their teasing and cutting remarks. She resisted wearing her glasses and would tuck them in a pocket or set them down somewhere. Many pairs became lost or broken. These factors were already hampering her ability to concentrate and learn.

In the spring of her first grade year, Sierra Leonean friends lived with us for two and a half months while establishing themselves in America. Their daughters became our children's instant same-aged playmates. Besides these friends and others at our church, Suzanne found a buddy in Heather New, who moved in across the street. The girls thought it uncanny that they were both adopted, and shared the same middle name and the same birthday (Heather is one year older).

During these years, Suzanne sang with a city-wide International Children's Choir. She loved singing, displaying the colors of her country's flag in her blue, white, and green African outfit. Many of the choir members were adopted or otherwise aware of their family backgrounds, and each wore a costume showing heritage.

It was very important to us that our children be made aware of their birth stories as soon as they could understand. We had heard of adolescents being overwhelmed when news of their adoption compounded the confusion of their teen years. There would be no surprises if we could help it. God had put our family together, and our kids were very special to us. We freely expressed this to them and others.

After a particular performance of the children's choir, an elderly woman asked about Suzanne. "She stands out from the others in her natural ability to perform," she commented. "I hope you will find ways to develop her dramatic and musical talents." Suzanne definitely exhibited both abilities, frequently singing at home while acting out her dramatic flair. I'm not sure if it was further drama, but sometime during her first grade year she decided that she was "Suzy," the name she began using on all school papers.

The overall experience of her first two years at school was not very positive. We considered looking elsewhere. Then a surprising event further challenged our family, convincing us of the need to pursue Christian education. We began inquiring about possibilities.

9

The Little Man

"Mom, the Snake is talking to me, but I'm not going to listen," five-year-old Suzy stated as we shopped for groceries together. I had asked her to choose some apples and put them in a bag, "Carefully, so they don't get bruised." She said she would obey me and not the Snake, adding, "I'll put them in carefully." Suzy had learned that there is a devil who sometimes takes the form of a snake, as in the garden of Eden. At an early age she seemed to recognize the difference in the spiritual forces at work around her.

She recalls a stark memory from those early school years: "I woke up and saw thirty or forty little gnome-like men coming toward me. I screamed, backing myself up into the corner to get as far away from them as possible. My cousin, who was staying in the room, woke up to my screams and turned on the light, asking if I was okay. 'Yes,' I said, as the little men had disappeared. Even though I was still afraid, I eventually went back to sleep."

A year later, when she was seven years old, Suzy began talking about a little man who was in her mind. "The little man tells me to do bad," she said. "He sits down to watch TV with Satan, and they laugh at me when I don't do what they want." At the same time, as recorded in my journal, she was becoming increasingly unmanageable in back talk and disobedience.

An African friend suggested that demonic spirits might be troubling our daughter. This was a new and disturbing thought. We were advised to talk with Mr. Brown, who had experience recognizing and casting out demons. With much apprehension, we arranged a visit. Joe had been fasting and praying for answers to Suzanne's belligerence; he decided we should hear what Mr. Brown had to say. When we explained our plan to Suzanne, she also became anxious, saying, "Why are we going to somebody's house? I don't want to talk about the little man anymore."

After asking our pastor and his wife to pray, we put our misgivings aside and traveled two and a half hours to the Browns' home in northern Indiana. I was afraid we would face a high-powered, emotion-packed prayer that would scare everybody and maybe do more harm than good. Instead, while his wife played with our children, Mr. Brown asked to hear our story and related his own experiences in dealing with demonic powers.

Then he advised, "This is usually not a deep-seated problem in a child, yet it needs to be addressed. I could pray over her and confront whatever demons might be troubling her, but to avoid trauma, it would be better to do this while she is sleeping. You, her parents, have the greatest authority over your child, so you are the best ones to determine if there is an evil spirit troubling her. If you believe there is, you can command it to leave by the power you have in Jesus Christ."

At his suggestion, we met late on a Thursday evening with four Christian friends. As we talked and prayed, we all became convinced of the need to boldly ask God's intervention for our sleeping children. After our pastor offered a simple prayer, Joe commanded the little man to leave, along with any other spirits that might be troubling our family. We claimed our home for Christ, rededicating it to Him. Recently Suzanne told us that, although she was asleep, she saw us that night as if she were above her body and watching.

A week later, she was once again talking about the little man. She agreed that Joe should repeat his command in Jesus' name that the little man must leave her alone. Then she added, "Dad, while you were telling the little man to leave, he was trying to talk to me, but I told him to leave too. I want Jesus in my heart!"

It was a memorable day: June 5, 1992. Twenty-seven years earlier on that day, Joe had made the decision to invite Jesus into his life.

We began seeing a changed person, a seven-year-old still needing correction, but the old belligerence was gone. I wondered if it was my imagination that she showed a new freedom and joy. No, she was truly set free from demonic power. We couldn't stop praising God for His gentle leadership.

Not long after this occurrence, Suzanne told us of a dream in which she saw Jesus holding out His hands to her. He said He wanted her to help her people in Africa. What was God's plan for this "little lost angel"?

10

Life's a Trap

We would love to state that our struggles were over and everything was rosy from that day on. You know... They lived happily ever after. One huge problem had been solved, with the result that Suzanne had firsthand understanding of the spirit world. She became very sensitive to the presence of evil. Yet this didn't change the attitudes of others toward her "different" appearance.

We opted for a local Christian school, even though Suzanne had to repeat first grade. However, the new atmosphere didn't change her feelings about herself or the stares and comments of others. Learning continued to be extremely difficult under the constant bombardment of her feelings of rejection. Soon she was enrolled in a special program within the school, educational therapy for "children with learning differences."

Suzy worked with a therapist whom she knew truly cared for her and wanted to help her. But her struggle for normalcy remained. In the spring of her fourth grade year, the principal asked to meet with us. She advised that Suzy was not making progress as expected. Then she added the shocking news that the school could no longer meet Suzy's needs, and she didn't know of any Christian school that could!

Joe and I had become committed to Christian education. We felt trapped. Where would we find the solution to this new, disturbing information? Yet it wasn't the first time we had seemed to be "backed into a corner" with no viable options. We sought God's guidance for this new cloudy chapter of our lives.

Without belaboring the story of Suzy's education, I will simply state that we spent an enriching year of home-schooling with both children. I chose the curriculum and taught four days a week. Joe took off work on Thursdays to give me a break, using a completely different approach from mine, including field trips and movie-making. Of course Suzy and Peter were the stars of their film. After that year our church started its own Christian school, and the children and I became involved in this new venture.

Suzy's problems were becoming more complex, each situation building on the former, heightened even more by the approach of adolescence. Craving the chance to be like the other girls in her class, she developed a pattern of dependence on those she deemed smart or beautiful. Her attention was now totally focused on gaining their affirmation.

Suzy as a ten-year-old

"I can't forgive God, who made me look this way," she proclaimed, "and I can't forgive the people who have stared at me and made mean comments about me." My suggestion that she was only hurting herself by holding a grudge brought the adamant claim, "I can't forgive!"

Suzanne felt very lonely. She had a few friends who encouraged her, claiming that she was beautiful, talented, and worthwhile, and suggesting that she seek the right companions and work hard to succeed in school. She had friends at church, but sadly, she felt rejected by others. In the midst of these confusing messages, her only happiness came through music, but the music she listened to was dark and had a negative effect on her.

She began to think she could find the acceptance she craved in a satanic cult. She told us years later that she was making definite plans to join, but she didn't have the funds that were needed. God was once again protecting our daughter.

We took Suzy to a Christian counselor, an "expert" in teen issues. He tried alternately to be her advocate and then make her angry. He teased her that she must actually be Egyptian, the "Queen of De-Nile." No matter what he tried, she wouldn't open up to him. Her confusion about identity had reached a climax. At age fourteen, and unable to focus on academics, she was failing seventh grade for the second time. Her academic, social, and spiritual lives all seemed headed to a dead end.

She summed up her feelings in a poem:

The Truth about Me

The truth about me is I'm a sinner ready to coil
I have a friendship within with no real one to show
I believe in God and His love for me,
But I fret to say my life has no blessing.

"But wait," you say, "what about your birth
And that special baby God spared on this earth?"
"This life is a gift," some people might say,
"The gift one man gave on a cross that
unforgettable day."

Times have changed, feelings must come out
Of this worrisome heart filled with doubt
Doubt for my friends, doubt for my peers
Doubt for this body wet with my tears.

I get so confused, there are lies that I'm told
This pain that I'm feeling, this existence I hold.
What can I do? This life's a trap
I feel like a gerbil or unwanted rat.

I know what I'll do; I'll give my heart away
To some fresh and new person per se.

A person to cherish, someone to love,
A gift from the Father straight from above

One who will love me just as I am
Who'll stand right beside me and call me a friend.

Well, until that day comes, and these feelings run out
Of this heart filled with pain and this doubt,
I'll just say a prayer and endure this time
Until my beauty has come and good feelings unwind.

Crisis Coming to a Head

Rest in the LORD and wait patiently for Him.

—Psalm 37:7

11

Unthinkable

It was an October day when desperation made us ready to demand answers from Suzy's counselor. Something had to be done to help our daughter.

I recalled a summer Sunday evening church service. Suzanne was sitting alone while the rest of the teens gave glowing reports of their wonderful prayer times and great services at youth camp. She had attended camp previously, but a girl had made fun of her and she refused to go back. My heart ached for her to enjoy the positive and fun experiences she was missing, and I was having my own conversation with God: "Lord, by next year I want Suzanne to attend camp, enjoy it, and grow through it. Even more, may she be turned around and headed in the right direction—spiritually, socially, emotionally, and academically."

Yet on that October day I didn't think the answer would be quite so drastic! Her counselor described a ranch for troubled teens in Montana, suggesting, "Residential treatment is needed for Suzanne's healing to take place, and this is the only place I can recommend." We were stunned! Wide-ranging thoughts raced through our confused minds. How could we send our daughter away? And how could we ever find the resources for such a program? On the other hand, the situation in our family was becoming unbearable for all of us. Something had to be done. We had put ourselves in the hands of a counselor; should we not attempt to heed his advice?

By a month after the initial suggestion, we were convinced that Suzanne required residential treatment, even as our emotions were vacillating. We were dealing with the "unthinkable." But these facts remained:

(1) Suzanne was very unhappy at school and with us.
(2) Her relationship with her brother had totally deteriorated.
(3) She began saying to me, "I hate you." When I asked her why, she said, "We don't get along, and I don't like people I don't get along with."
(4) We were hearing deep sighs from our daughter.
(5) Her identity was definitely in limbo, even regarding her basic nationality and race.

We applied to the ranch, asking God's clear guidance and the necessary finances ($4500 per month!). Early in December, we were informed that the program would cost double the amount previously stated, and they could not enroll Suzanne at that time. Other facilities were recommended.

Inquiring about the nearest one, Shelterwood in Branson, Missouri, brought the credentials of the Shelterwood staff by return mail with news that the cost would be $3000 per month, but there was a waiting list. In those days one couldn't simply look up a website, and long-distance phone calls were costly. Although we were unable to learn more about the program, nor did we know when a spot might become available, we decided to apply. To our great surprise, an invitation to enroll Suzanne by the end of January 2000 came in just fifteen days. Believing it was God's answer, we began preparations.

As Suzy's counselor advised, we didn't tell her of our intention to take her to Shelterwood until two days before our planned trip to Branson. Her youth pastor, his wife, and a good friend from church, Heather Earnest, came to support her as she heard the news. She was annoyed that everyone else knew what was happening before she did.

Joe had carefully outlined the reasons for this extremely difficult decision, emphasizing that we loved her very much. We were surprised that the suggestion of residential treatment didn't elicit an angry response. Suzy was excited to see the suitcase full of new clothes and bedding we had purchased for her. Yet for two days she simply and quietly kept repeating, "I don't want to go." Recently she told me that she hadn't cared what we arranged; it wasn't real to her. She felt hopeless that anything could change.

Peter was confused about our proposal. "Even though Suzy gives me a bad time," he said, "I will really miss her. She's fun. Won't she be here for our birthdays?"

No, Peter, she won't.

12

Shelterwood

Someone has written, "Is your life a whirlwind and you're living on the edge of a scream? Difficulties and impossibilities set the stage for a miracle."

Our eight-hour journey to Branson that Monday was strained but uneventful. We left early, stopping for breakfast. Laughter lightened the mood as Suzy ordered "bacon," believing it to be the side order of eggs and toast. The waitress brought her a single small plate containing two slices of bacon, while Joe had three or four plates (the Farmer's Breakfast). "A great way to take care of your family, Dad!" we teased. Yet for most of the trip, Suzy sullenly enveloped herself in music in the backseat of our white Explorer.

We had not previously visited Branson. For many miles, billboards announced the various attractions in this tourist-popular town, but these held no interest for us. MapBlast! directed us up a hill east of the main thoroughfare to the modest Shelterwood campus. It reminded us of a camp with its rustic cabins housing the main office and those of professional counselors. A path led to the three-story boys' and girls' houses. Following the driveway down the hill behind the cabins, we visited the small school at the edge of the woods.

We were invited into one of the cozy cabins to meet with five of the staff members. They were Todd, the director; Dan, who was to be her counselor; Darcy, the girls' "house mother"; Aaron, headmaster of the private school; and the head counselor, Sheri. They interviewed Suzy, asking many questions, such as "Why do you think you're here?" "What problems have you been facing?" We listened with amazement as she responded to each query openly and accurately. There was nothing to add. When I asked Suzanne about this recently, she said she had just wanted to be heard.

Darcy took Suzanne on a tour of the grounds, while we met with Todd and Dan. Shelterwood, we learned, was so named because recent college graduates volunteered a year of their time to become sheltering "big brothers" or "sisters" to the teens enrolled in the program. Each "big" spent much of her or his time with three or four "littles," including sleeping in their rooms.

Todd explained the ten-month, five-level program. He confirmed the cost of $3000 per month at that time. "However," he said, "we have decided to defer half of your payment in appreciation for your ministry jobs." (Joe was working for our church headquarters and I was teaching at a Christian school.) God was leading us to trust our daughter to this ministry. He would provide for all of us in this new venture, meeting our financial and emotional needs.

The decision having been made, a simple good-bye was suggested to avoid a strained parting. At the girls' house, we found Suzanne unpacking her suitcase, gave her hugs, and were on our way. What agony! We wept as we began the painful trip back home without her. From deep within I felt a cry: "No! No! This can't be right! You can't take her away from us!" Yet, in some crazy way, these painful emotions were mixed with a sense of peace. God was working His purposes in all of our lives.

13

A Different Lifestyle

Everyone was staring and Suzy felt awkward, abandoned, confused, and angry. During her first day at Shelterwood, she had been introduced to all the teen and women staff members living in the girls' house. The next morning she walked with others to the private school down the hill to meet the teachers and the boys in the program. She quickly noted that only she and one of the male students were of black heritage. The girls were stylishly and femininely dressed, while she wore baggy pants and oversized T-shirts. She was the one out of place here! Within a few days, she learned that some of the teens had been involved in gangs, prostitution, or drugs. They seemed hard, and Suzanne felt intimidated by them. Her best plan, she thought, would be to make them afraid of her by mirroring their hard exteriors.

Suzy's housemother informed her of the requirements of the program. On level one she was not allowed her comfortable escape into music. Also she could not communicate with family or friends. To make matters worse, she couldn't be more than five feet from a staff member at all times. She couldn't even use the bathroom alone!

Suzy was assigned a daily room chore and house chore to be completed before the seven o'clock breakfast each morning, followed by the walk to school. During her first week, Suzanne and another new girl decided they would sleep in and not do chores. They soon learned the consequences: the two of them became responsible for the chores of all the girls. Before breakfast, they were expected to wash all windows, empty trash from all rooms, complete the laundry, and vacuum and dust the whole house, as well as put their own rooms in order. Every job was carefully monitored and redone as needed, while random cleanliness checks kept their rooms in shape. If they were late for breakfast, all the girls would be punished for their misdemeanor, and the offenders would be on "room grounding" each afternoon. This meant going straight from school to their individual rooms, sitting at their desks, and reading the Bible or a schoolbook (There was no sleeping during room grounding). They would have to help prepare the evening meal in the basement kitchen, but couldn't eat until everyone else had finished. Then they took their food back to their rooms, ate alone, and finally returned the dishes to the kitchen, washed them, and helped with other after-meal duties.

The girls learned that those who completed their chores well and with good attitudes were given points that could be used for treats during a trip to town. They would be involved in special “room” and “house” activities. Suzy decided she would do the assigned chores.

The privileges gradually increased. On level two, she was allowed to be fifteen feet from a staff member and could communicate with us weekly by phone during a specified half-hour time slot. She could also receive notes from a selected list of friends.

Level three allowed her to enjoy approved Christian music through headphones, and she was no longer restricted to constant staff surveillance. This level involved two big assignments that Suzanne was sure she would never accomplish: telling her life story and leading a study she would prepare for members of the girls’ house, including women staff members. The first three levels, scheduled to last three to four months, took Suzanne more than a year. She was being “opened up” as a person and finding it very difficult. There was no longer opportunity to hide behind Mom and Dad.

During that lengthy period, her counselor recommended a wilderness boot camp for Suzanne because she wouldn’t cooperate. She had heard about boot camps and definitely didn’t want that. Also Joe insisted, “I don’t want you to give up on Suzy. She needs the success of finishing the program.”

At long last Suzy achieved the stated goals and moved on to level four. Then on a fall day when many of the girls were chatting on the veranda, Sheri brought the news. Suzy had reached the final level! There was much cheering, hugs, and tears among the girls. She had accomplished her goals at last, and her friends rejoiced with her! She could go off the property by herself or with others who had reached the same level. She could also phone her friends whenever she wished.

By the time of her graduation twenty-two months after starting the program, none of the teens whom she had met upon arriving at Shelterwood still remained on campus. A few of the "littles" who had graduated returned for this special occasion, as well as her first "big sister," Becca, who had borne the brunt of Suzy's early days of total defiance. All the girls circled around the graduate on the basketball court for leisurely expressions of their shared experiences.

Not until then did we learn many of the things that had happened. Yes, some had been afraid of her, but they concluded that she was "mushy-hard." The real Suzanne cared very much about others; they had learned to understand and love her. Many stated their appreciation of her input of Scripture into almost any discussion. They also spoke of her determination. A favorite story involved a girls' football game in which Suzy grabbed the ball and raced for the goal. Five players tackled her, but she wouldn't be held back. She continued on, dragging them down the field.

Her graduation ceremony brought another surprise. Suzy, who had always been afraid of the stares of others, stood before parents, staff, and teens to sing a solo: "Thank you for giving to the Lord; I am a life that was changed."[5] She had grown in so many ways. She had also made a new commitment to the Lord.

When we first considered Shelterwood, "friends" had said, "There are no guarantees. You may be throwing away your retirement by choosing residential treatment." The cost *was* huge! With the deferment, there were forty-four months of $1500 payments, a staggering $66,000. We couldn't explain how, but the correct amount was paid by each due date. With financial help from others providing less than one month's cost, Joe was given overtime work, and God, according to His promise to supply our needs, made up the difference.

Was it worth the effort, agony, and financial output? Yes! Shelterwood didn't solve all of Suzy's problems, but she claims that her experience there saved her life and prepared her for meeting her birth family and her future husband.

New Beginnings

Dwell in the land and cultivate faithfulness.

—Psalm 37:3

14

Suzy's Great Big Family

"Wait a minute. That was one of your [African] cousins!" The statement surprised us all! Rev. J. Y. Conteh, visiting from Sierra Leone, had just phoned an acquaintance living in the States. Then he recalled the connection to Suzanne. She called right back, excited to talk with her cousin, Sassa Mansaray.

It had been two years since Suzy's return from Shelterwood. In that time she finished school and was working at a grocery store deli. Over the next few months she connected with other relatives and visited them in Philadelphia, Chicago, and Seattle. Without realizing it, Suzy was beginning the process of sorting out her identity. She was learning to accept herself as the beautiful woman God had created her to be.

In January 2005, eighteen years after our return to the States, Suzy and I traveled to Africa. We had talked of this trip for many years; she needed to experience the land and people of Sierra Leone. The visit would challenge her in many ways, starting with the thirty-six-hour journey to London and on to Freetown, the capital city of Sierra Leone. Yet we couldn't have guessed how drastically life-changing this trip would be!

Lungi Airport sits on a peninsula across the bay from Freetown. One can travel from there by land to the interior of the country, but it would be more than a day's car trip to the capital. The better choice is vintage helicopter across the inlet. We strained for our first glimpse of Freetown through clouded portholes and an aircraft packed with travelers.

J. Y. and his wife, Adema, anxiously awaited our arrival. Six of Suzy's African uncles also came to welcome her! "That was overwhelming, but exciting!" she exclaimed. Her closest uncle, Mohammed Baba Kamara, who had represented the family during her adoption process, was employed by the police department. His boss, the inspector general, loaned us his new Land Rover and driver for the duration of our sojourn. I felt like I was accompanying royalty.

Our longtime friends, Philip and Sallay Sesay, had prepared rooms in the home of another uncle, Samuel Baio Kamara, on the Jui Bible College campus. We arrived at our quarters around two that morning. As we prepared for bed, Suzy urged, "Mom, can I sleep with you?"

Surprised, I asked, "Why, what are you afraid of?"

"Bugs."

Nets hung around the beds would help ward off mosquitoes, but she had seen a spider on the wall. Suzy's panic at the sight of insects of all kinds brought anxiety added to weariness. We slept little, and our jet-lagged eyes popped open when a chorus of birds loudly welcomed the day in the trees outside the levered windows.

In the candlelight of the night before, we had not noticed the bathtub full of clean water and a brimming bucket nearby. It was dry season and water had to be preserved since pressure was low here at the end of the pipeline. "Where do I take my shower?" Suzy asked. I couldn't help laughing as I informed her of the "bucket shower" with cold water and a dipper.

In spite of numerous adjustments, Suzy enjoyed the trip immensely, especially being introduced to African relatives. As she was growing up, we had noticed her desire for a large family. She counted and memorized information about some thirty American cousins and second cousins. Then she claimed many more, rehearsing their ages and birth dates.

Now a seemingly endless stream of visitors stated their claim as Suzy's "family." The people of her native village were mainly Mansarays and Kamaras. Suzy's birthfather was a Mansaray, and her birthmother was part of the Kamara clan. Because there were many Kamaras and Sassa was a common name, her birthmother was also known by her mother's name: Sassa Yamie Kamara.

In a broad sense, anyone born in Bafodia was part of her extended family. Older relatives were called “uncle” or “auntie”; anyone near her age or younger would be brother, sister, or cousin. No matter where we traveled in the country, visitors approached, saying, “I’m your auntie” or “I’m your cousin.” She loved it!

Suzy at twenty, ready for adventure.

15

Uncovering Roots

The five-hour trip from Freetown to Kabala left us in darkness as we continued our journey bouncing over the rugged final twenty miles to Suzy's birth-village. Even before our arrival, we had noticed unexpected lights in this out-of-the-way place. A single small generator was powering light bulbs on three or four verandas, including the cement-block house where we finally stopped, dust-covered and weary. In spite of the late hour, our Land Rover was quickly surrounded. The news of Suzy's coming had spread, and many were anxious to see the one born in their midst twenty years earlier.

Among them was a woman who spoke excellent English. She introduced Suzy to her half-brother and sister, younger children of her birthfather. Fatmata Mansaray had firsthand knowledge of Suzanne's heritage; she had been a friend of Suzy's birthmother and was on hand for the birth of Sassa's diminutive twins. Some years later, Suzy was reminded of this encounter when she learned that Fatmata Mansaray was her future mother-in-law.

Sadly, she died in a car accident before Suzy ever met her husband-to-be.

The section chief, another uncle, Alimamy Hamidu I, welcomed us, and we were taken to comfortable quarters at his home. Half of the large room was overtaken by a king-sized wooden bed complete with homemade quilt, reminiscent of those crafted by church ladies in the States for mission use. Suzy had come "home" to a strangely inviting place. We were intrigued, finding it hard to sleep as we considered what the new day would bring.

Harmattan, that cold wind that blows south from the Sahara, had come once again. The morning dawned cool to roosters crowing and the excited voices of children. Our earliest visitors came to our veranda, shivering in the chilled dryness and anxiously awaiting another sight of the recently arrived guests. But we needed showers after the dusty ride of the night before. Though she was now familiar with bucket-and-dipper showers, Suzy was not prepared for the chilly outdoor "room" boasting a pebbled floor and woven grass walls but no roof. Nearby, the plaited fence enclosed a rare sight, an outhouse with a seat!

Soon we were touring Bafodia, situated near the forest with hills beyond on all sides. For me, memories flooded back of this place that appeared virtually unchanged since our last visit almost two decades before, while Suzy paid rapt attention to the village she had heard of all her life. The children had waited patiently and now followed closely, not wanting to miss anything Suzy said or did. A few public buildings could be seen near the town's center: the tall church, with its simple benches and pulpit, the nearby mosque, and the Court Barrie, an open structure containing a small room and large "porch," where public meetings or occasional clinics by visiting missionaries were held. The elementary school with simple glassless window openings and rough desks stood to the south toward the Kabala road.

Most homes were constructed of mud blocks dried in the sun, then stacked with wet sticky dirt or mortar (when available) and sticks or boards between for stability. Roofs of these rounded one-room dwellings were invariably made of bundled dried grass. The kitchen was outside in back—a cooking pot supported by three large stones over a wood fire.

A few more affluent residences sported cement block walls and roofs of corrugated tin, like the one where we lodged. These held a central sitting room surrounded by bedrooms or storage areas, all heated by the tropical sun beating down on the shiny metal. Grass-roofed dwellings had cooler interiors but allowed in many more tiny unwanted inhabitants!

By late morning we were invited to a veranda across the lane from our house for an official welcome, translated for us from the Limba language. Pastor Philip responded with a speech of appreciation on our behalf. Gifts of rice, peanuts, and fruit were set before us. These, along with two live chickens, would be cooked for our meals during our brief stay. I had advised Suzy that if given a chicken she would be expected to hold it as a gesture of acceptance and gratitude. Another new experience.

We stood before the grave of Suzy's twin brother at the edge of the forest, not far from the now broken-down, mud-block home where they had been born. At less than three pounds and without his mother, the baby boy had lived only one day. Later, at the other end of the village, down the hill from the mission house, we viewed the burial place of Suzy's birthmother. At Joe's request, Larry Marshall had ensured that both graves could be located by preparing cement coverings for them. We became pensive as we considered all we knew about this courageous woman, Sassa Kamara.

Suzy later reflected,

> The trip to Sierra Leone was a crossroads in my life. It was like history being revisited and also being made. I felt like I was an American when I left home, but now I'm African. My goal was just to see my birth country, but meeting so many of my family members gave me new understanding of myself, with an overwhelming sense of responsibility to help them as I can. It made me grateful for my life in the States and for my adoptive parents. I was surprised how much our return meant to the people

> of Bafodia. Many expressed that they had thought of me often, wondering what was happening with me and praying for me. They didn't think they would ever see me again. Overall, I feel I have a better handle on my identity because of experiencing my roots.

The other major event of the trip was Suzanne being noticed by Ansu Kamara.

Unexpected Destiny

He will give you the desires of your heart.

—Psalm 37:4

16

"I Want Her; I Want to Marry Her"

"Do you know who that person is?" Ansu's friend asked him as they noticed a blonde woman in the passing vehicle.

"No. Who is she?"

"You know, Auntie Sassa Yamie's child that the missionaries took to America."

Ansu's heart was stirred with the memory of a tiny baby born in his village twenty years earlier and with thoughts of her beauty.

It was much later that we learned of these events and understood that Providence was at work. It had been the second day of our roots trip. After attending the church that Philip pastors in Freetown, we expected Barrie, our driver, to take us to lunch and then on the long trip to Bafodia. The tropical sun beat down as we waited . . . and waited. Finally, Pastor Philip took us to his home; we would catch up with our driver later. It was as we left the church that Ansu noticed Suzy.

In the intervening years Ansu had completed his high school education. He obtained a diploma in business studies and a certificate in computer software. He would soon work as an administrative assistant for a construction company in Freetown. But he could not get the beautiful woman he had seen off his mind.

When Suzy's cousin P. B. K. visited Ansu in Freetown, he suggested that Ansu might consider learning more about someone named Suzanne, who had recently rejoined the family. Ansu commented that he had already seen her and was very interested. Their mothers had been best friends; Ansu's mother and grandmother had been on hand when Suzanne and her twin brother were born. He was attracted to her and soon declared, "I want her; I want to marry her."

Back in the States, various men were pursuing Suzy. It would seem that she'd be in danger of giving in to these attentions, even as she had expressed:

> I know what I'll do; I'll give my heart away
> To some fresh and new person per se.

She was still living at home with us and visiting African relatives living in various American cities. As she told us of her experiences and of men who had shown an interest in her, we realized that God was giving her wisdom and discernment that overshadowed her vulnerability. She was saving her heart for a special individual:

A person to cherish, someone to love
A gift from the Father straight from above
One who will love me just as I am
Who'll stand right beside me and call me a friend.

Six months after our "roots" trip, during an African family reunion in Chicago, P.B.K. and another family member, Mosiray Balla Kuyateh, who we know as Jacky, made a phone call to Africa. They told Suzy that someone wanted to talk with her. It was a brief conversation with Ansu Kamara, but he promised to call her again.

Ansu's uncle Alpha was at the reunion, and he suggested that Suzy might think about getting to know Ansu. They had much in common, he noted. Both were born in the same village and both had lost their mothers, hers at her birth and Ansu's more recently in a vehicle accident. The phones buzzed with discussions across the ocean. As the couple began getting to know one another, Suzy was attracted to the voice on the phone, and soon Ansu stated his wishes to Suzanne: "I would like to have an everlasting relationship with you."

Suzy's initial response was, "We can talk!" But the next day she announced to us that she was going to marry him.

She realized how important it was for her to marry a man from her village—one who could teach their children the culture and language of her birth family. She also wanted to show respect to the memory of her birthmother by carrying on her name and bloodline as part of the

Limba tribe. Uncle Alpha's words hit home and she agreed to the proposal. Her conclusion was, "Why not go for it? I only have one life to live." She now believes that God was guiding her decision.

Ansu was a total unknown to Joe and me. Who was he? Why did he want to marry our daughter? How could we find out about him? We decided to ask our friend Pastor Philip to "check him out."

When the meeting finally occurred, Philip began his inquiry with the culturally appropriate statement: "Suzy is my daughter. What are your intentions?" After a long interview with many pointed questions, he asked to meet Ansu's father, and another session was planned. Finally Philip concluded, "I believe Suzanne should marry an African and that he should be from her village. I give my blessing to this union." We knew Philip cared very much for us and Suzanne. His words were the confirmation we needed to believe that this marriage was in God's plan.

Lengthy discussions continued between the couple, via expensive phone cards, for the next two years. They were talking at every opportunity, five or six times a day. Often it was the middle of the night for Suzy, which was early morning for Ansu.

Suzy commented, "The frequent calls were necessary. Without them, it's too easy to wonder what the other person is doing and whether they really care. I didn't want any surprises when we finally met," she added, "so I shared all the details about myself—the good, the bad, and the ugly. I wanted someone who would know all about me and still love me in spite of my struggles and imperfections. We told each other everything we did and everywhere we went, plus anything that happened. We didn't want to hear news from someone else about what the other was doing."

Conversations covered the seriousness of marriage and beliefs about childrearing. Ansu had been raised in a polygamist home and he didn't want that lifestyle for his children. For him it would be one and only one wife.

Both were agreed about Christianity. Ansu had decided in grade school that he wanted to be a Christian, and Suzy had made commitments to the Lord as a child and again during her years at Shelterwood.

Then there were thoughts about the future, wondering when they would be able to meet and marry and what plans they would make for a family and career. They were growing in their knowledge of and commitment to one another.

17

"May We Pick a Rose?"

I remembered back to Saturday, the last day of our "roots trip." While Suzy and I were sleeping in, busy activity was occurring at Philip and Sallay's home across the Bible college campus. Large pots were bubbling over three-stone fires in the kitchen area behind their house. Women were busy cutting onions; opening cans of tomato paste; preparing fish, beef, and hot peppers; pouring palm oil; and beating rice to remove the husks for the celebration Jollof rice. Shrimp chips, soft drinks, ginger beer (a stronger version of ginger ale), and deep-fried cakes would complete the meal for the eighty to a hundred expected attendees.

By early afternoon guests began arriving for the engagement ceremony of Pastor Philip's niece. Relatives of the "bride" could be identified by their "ashobie": men's shirts and women's gowns and head wraps all made of the same blue fabric. As many family and friends as possible crowded into the living room, while the use of a microphone included in the proceedings those sitting outside.

Philip's niece was visiting family in the States, so his daughter Priscilla would stand in for her absent cousin. The couple didn't both need to be present, we learned, because betrothal is a contract not only between individuals but between families. Suzanne and I watched the activities with growing interest.

I had learned of the ritual soon after we first arrived in Sierra Leone twenty-seven years earlier, but had only previously witnessed one engagement by video. It involves a drama acted out as if no one knows what's happening, although all has been prearranged. Time is immaterial and each step involves long and humorous discussions.

The bride's family had finally gathered as the afternoon approached four o'clock. Then, at last, the relatives of the intended groom arrived. Unlike this open culture where even strangers are welcomed to one's home, the visitors were kept standing outside until they could clearly state their intentions: "We have seen a beautiful rose in your garden and would like permission to pick it."

Through much banter and the passing of token amounts of money, the visitors were eventually crowded into the already overflowing room. Then, a "rose" (a lovely young girl) was presented and admired but tactfully passed over with regrets as the family sought the "right rose." Priscilla entered the room, beautifully dressed and covered with a filmy white scarf, to be claimed as the desired rose. She was queried about her acceptance of the marriage proposal and more speeches and gifts followed. The new bride (when she returned from the States) would now go and live in her groom's home, learning from her mother-in-law. Finally everyone shared in the meal of celebration.

A year later, Joe and I were hosting Suzanne's engagement, although she had still not personally met Ansu. Many friends, former missionaries, and relatives gathered in a double-sized schoolroom. A cousin, Mohamed Bah, stood in for Ansu, who was still in Africa, and four of Suzy's young friends plus a surprise guest were chosen to be the "roses."

Per custom, Ansu's family members—led by Uncle Musa Mansaray from Chicago, the head of the U.S. section of the family—were kept outside the door until they clearly stated their wish: to pick a rose. The banter had begun and would continue without regard to time. Two beautifully dressed girls were ushered in, one at a time, and duly admired but passed over. Then our family spokesman announced that the next rose had been given much special attention and was a real prize. Mrs. Lois Sawyer entered the room covered in a veil and using a walker. When the crowd cheered, she shook the walker in response, bringing more applause and laughter.

The last two lovely roses were presented. Then Suzy was escorted into the room, her head and shoulders well covered in opaque lace. The banter continued, requesting removal of the veil for complete assurance that this was the desired rose. Finally her hair and then her face were revealed to much acclaim by the crowd.

Suzy spoke her agreement to the match, and further speeches accompanied gifts from Ansu's family. These exhibited special traditional meaning: a calabash (a hollowed-out gourd) used in food preparation, a needle and thread for mending his clothes, a cola nut (previously used for currency and now to show respect), a mat on which the couple could sleep, a white cloth for purity, a large family Bible, and money for an engagement ring. Suzy was invited to sit on the mat, and the Sierra Leonean women danced around her, singing about the bride in the native Limba language. Finally all were invited to a celebration dinner of African and American foods. Thus Suzanne Renee Estes became engaged to Alimamy Ansu Kamara on January 21, 2006.

18

They Meet

April 2006 stands out in our family for major changes in various relationships, including the passing of Joe's sister after a long bout with cancer and the news of a grandchild on the way. Another big change was Suzy's move to Philadelphia. We took her to spend a month with her cousins P. B. K. and Jane, but she ended up staying for much longer, also spending time with her cousin Sassa Mansaray and her husband Kebbie Turay. This was a major step in her cultural understanding and another huge learning curve for Suzanne. It brought further progress toward defining her identity, and she claims it was necessary preparation for her upcoming marriage.

The application for Ansu's fiancé visa was submitted on April 4, but we heard nothing until that October. The visa was denied, we learned, because of "lack of evidence of their engagement," despite letters written by witnesses to the ceremony. Immigration wanted pictures as proof that the couple had actually met.

Thus Suzanne planned a trip to Freetown for April 2007. It was just over two years since Ansu had seen her and began to state that he wanted to marry her. Their relationship had grown through extended conversations across the ocean.

It seemed that evil forces were actively at work, using people and orchestrating circumstances to disrupt their plans. During the week she was to leave for Sierra Leone, Suzy's passport and photo ID both came up missing. She looked everywhere, but they were not to be found. P. B. K had already helped Suzanne in many ways, and he agreed to go with her to the embassy in downtown Philadelphia. After a long day of waiting, she was promised the new passport, which arrived in the mail just a few days later. However, P. B. K.'s car was towed, they had to take a taxi across town, he was late for work, and he missed an appointment. It was a costly and time-consuming process. A phone call to the airport confirmed that a Social Security card along with the passport would suffice in place of an ID.

Finally Suzy and P. B. K. were on their way, flying out of New York to London, where they spent the night with Sierra Leonean family members before continuing on to Freetown. She felt that she already knew Ansu through their multiple phone conversations and was very excited but also a bit nervous to meet him in person. Yet when the airport helicopter landed, he was nowhere to be seen. Only an uncle and her cousin's wife met them. Ansu had hidden, wanting to surprise her. Suddenly he was there, giving her a red rose with a note telling of his joy at finally meeting her in person.

They meet.

Throughout the next twenty-two days of her visit, Suzy felt a wide range of emotions. She shared these thoughts:

> As soon as I saw Ansu I felt comfortable. It was real joy to finally be with him and share with him in person. He was all I thought he would be and more. Being together brought a new dimension to our relationship.
>
> I was excited to experience so much that was new and different in the bustling city of Freetown. The streets and sidewalks were filled with people, many of them carrying food or other items for sale on their heads. The smell of wood fires mingled with frying foods, the hot tropical air, and exhaust from the seemingly endless stream of traffic.
>
> Daylight extends for twelve hours year round in the tropics, and night comes on very quickly around seven o'clock. There were no streetlights in Freetown at that time. With my poor vision, I had trouble seeing, even with a flashlight, as we walked through the crowded streets. I almost fell into a large pothole, but thankfully Ansu caught me before I fell. Back at the house we used a generator for part of the evening and then, to save fuel, resorted to kerosene lamps.

We went to see Ansu's father. As a member of parliament, the Honorable Philipson Humaru Kamara owned a large home near the stadium, not far from the beach. The sitting room was filled with family, including two of Ansu's stepmothers and many of his brothers and sisters. I felt acceptance and a strange affinity to them, although shy and nervous at meeting so many new people. Yet there was a certain detachment. I had not shared their lives and memories: I was an outsider. While living in Philadelphia, I had been learning Krio, the English-based trade language of Sierra Leone. Upon meeting Ansu's father I said, "Ah lek yu pikin too mos" (I really like your son!). He was amused and somewhat taken aback but responded that he was happy to meet me. He asked Ansu if he had decided about me. When Ansu declared that he had, his father warned him that any change in that decision would bring shame on the family. He had better be sure of his plans.

The acceptance and love shown by Ansu's sister, Sarah, was very touching. Without refrigeration available, she brought breakfast every morning of my stay: eggs, bread, and fruit to enjoy with hot chocolate. We were usually out visiting people during the day or enjoying the beautiful beach of the Atlantic coast. By the time we returned to the house, Sarah had left our evening meal—the staple rice with cassava or potato leaf cooked with fish, beef, or chicken (or a combination of these) in a base of palm oil, tomato paste, and onions. At other times it was a peanut-butter-based sauce over rice, or beans with similar ingredients. Hot pepper, enjoyed by most Sierra Leoneans, was lessened in deference to this American's taste. I had become used to these foods during my stay in Philadelphia and thoroughly enjoyed the abundant meals. Leftovers were invariably shared with others living in the house and around the compound.

My cousin Abbie came daily, in spite of a three-mile walk, to pick up my laundry. She carried it home to wash by hand and returned it the next day, clean and neatly folded.

We visited many more people, including members of my birth-family. I felt sad that I was not able to meet my birthparents. It had been twenty-two years since my mother, Sassa Kamara, died just after giving birth; and my father, Saiyo Mansaray, passed away

> during Sierra Leone's long civil war. I met two of my birth dad's sisters and reconnected with the half-brother I had seen in Bafodia. The poverty I saw all around me, even within my own family, brought pain and determination to do what I could to help them.
>
> In spite of the strangeness, somehow this city and her people were intriguingly part of who I am. Our meetings were characterized by loud conversations and much laughter. This helped my comfort level as I have always loved to laugh. I didn't know at that time about the extremely complicated relationships that exist among Sierra Leone's people.

An important experience took place when Suzy and Ansu attended a large church in Freetown. Suzy related, "The pastor was praying against evil spirits and demonic forces. People were going to the front of the church to pray, but I have never liked having someone pray over me. Then an usher touched our shoulders and suggested that we go forward for prayer. At the front, the pastor laid his hands on us and said, 'I sense that God has a plan for you two and there is a woman who is trying to fight you. She doesn't want you to succeed. But you will be able to go to America and God will use you for His purposes.' This was great confirmation of God's plan for us."

19

The Waiting Game

The day came for Suzanne to return to the States. Ansu escorted her to the plane, but he couldn't go right home to a normal routine. He spent two days in the airport thinking about her visit and the future. It had been so wonderful to finally be with Suzy. He loved introducing her to his family and friends. They talked on an even deeper level than possible by phone. But doubts and questions came rushing in: "Will it last? Will I ever see her again? Will she get tired of waiting for visa approval?" Phone calls increased after her return, with plans for his coming to the States uppermost in their minds.

Another year passed. It was spring 2008 before Ansu finally received word that, except for a physical, he was cleared to get a visa. He needed to travel to Senegal because the embassy in Freetown, destroyed during the ten-year civil war, was still under construction. This involved more expense and more waiting. Ansu passed his physical; then Alben, the young man with whom he was staying, accompanied him to the embassy.

It surprised Ansu that he was first to be invited into the office, although many others were waiting their turn. Then he was dismayed to hear, "The fees have changed. You need another hundred dollars to get your visa, and we can only give you two hours to find the money." Once again it seemed that an enemy was fighting to keep the couple apart.

When Ansu shared this news with Alben, he replied, "Wait. I have $35. It's a start, and you will be able to get the rest." Ansu called his uncle Kemoh Mansaray, who was living in England. His uncle sent funds immediately through Western Union. Further help came from a taxi driver who took Ansu and his friend to the Western Union office and back but refused to accept payment for his service.

As Ansu approached the embassy once again, he saw the woman in charge watching him from the window, and he was ushered directly into her office. With the correct funds in hand and all papers in order, the visa was promised for Friday, two days later.

Ansu received the documents and planned to return to Freetown to say "proper goodbyes" to his family. However, he learned that his plane was broken down and there wasn't another one to replace it. During the next month Ansu checked for the flight again and again, but was told that repairs were still not complete. On the phone Suzy said, "Just come!" Then he remembered his grandmother advising him, "If you get clearance, don't return to Freetown. Go directly to America." Suzy and her uncle Alpha Mansaray had contributed the funds for his ticket; Ansu picked it up at the airport and was on his way to the U.S. via Atlanta and finally New York.

Alimamy Ansu Kamara in 2008

20

Wedding

Joe and I were excitedly heading to the Indianapolis airport to pick up Suzy and Ansu. Finally, burdened with travel bags, they trudged down the long hallway to the security line where we waited. How wonderful to finally meet Ansu face to face! It was July 8, 2008. He had arrived in Philadelphia only nine days earlier and, in consultation with the African family, a wedding was already scheduled for July 27 at our church. Wow! Less than three weeks to complete all the arrangements.

Plans began to fall into place, with attendants chosen, a reception hall and caterer procured, a friend planning to make the beautiful cake, decorations donated by another friend married earlier that month, and many other details.

I was particularly concerned that Suzy still didn't have a bridal gown, and I anxiously prayed, "Lord, we *can't* have a wedding without a wedding dress!" Quickly the thought came clearly to mind: "I'm keeping one for you, dear." How wonderful! He is our Provider as well as our Peace. I was able to relax in the knowledge that God would "keep" the right gown for Suzy. And He did! She tried various dresses, but her eyes lit up as soon as she saw the "one"—a lovely ivory gown with floor-length lace jacket. It was just right!

Everything was new for Ansu. We enjoyed watching his enthusiasm as he was fitted for tuxedo and shoes. He wanted his to match the bride's outfit and queried us about the black clothing he tried on for sizing. "Yes," we confirmed, "yours will be ivory."

We had become acquainted with Rev. James Moorehead, the pastor of a local church and professor at nearby Anderson University. He has dealt with albinism all his life and seemed to feel a special affinity for Suzanne. He gladly agreed to counsel the couple and perform their wedding.

Finally the special day arrived. Everything was arranged and the church beautifully decorated by our creative friend, Kay Heer, with help from others. The lavish gowns and head wraps of the African family added color and interest to the occasion, along with the lovely decorations and blue-and-ivory-clad bridal party. Suzy's niece was the flower girl and her nephew a handsome little ring-bearer.

Suzy and Ansu were excited, laughing a lot during the day. In repeating the vows, Ansu said "I do" every time the pastor paused!

Rev. Moorehead suggested including the ritual of "jumping the broom" at the close of the wedding ceremony.

He explained that it had signified the commitment of a bride and groom when no legal marriage was recognized for slaves in the early days of our country. After he introduced Mr. and Mrs. Ansu Kamara, they jumped the broom that had been laid in front of them and happily marched out to greet their guests.

A reception was held in a large room at the nearby 4H fairgrounds. Many expressed how beautiful the occasion was, and I heard "princess bride" more than once. A highlight was Cindy Marshall telling the story of Suzanne's birth. My sister Joy had prepared a very special gift—a painting representing Suzy's birthmother. She was shown wearing green, blue, and white, the colors of the Sierra Leone flag, and holding her tiny twin babies—one with dark skin and hair and the other blonde with white skin. The tear in her eye touched all of us with the sadness she must have felt for her offspring. The painting was displayed along with a picture of Ansu's mother, also deceased. On this happy wedding day we believed they both would have been joyful over the union of their daughter and son.

The wonderful event ended all too soon. We were worn out and rested while the couple spent a three-night honeymoon in downtown Indianapolis. Soon they were on their way back to Philadelphia.

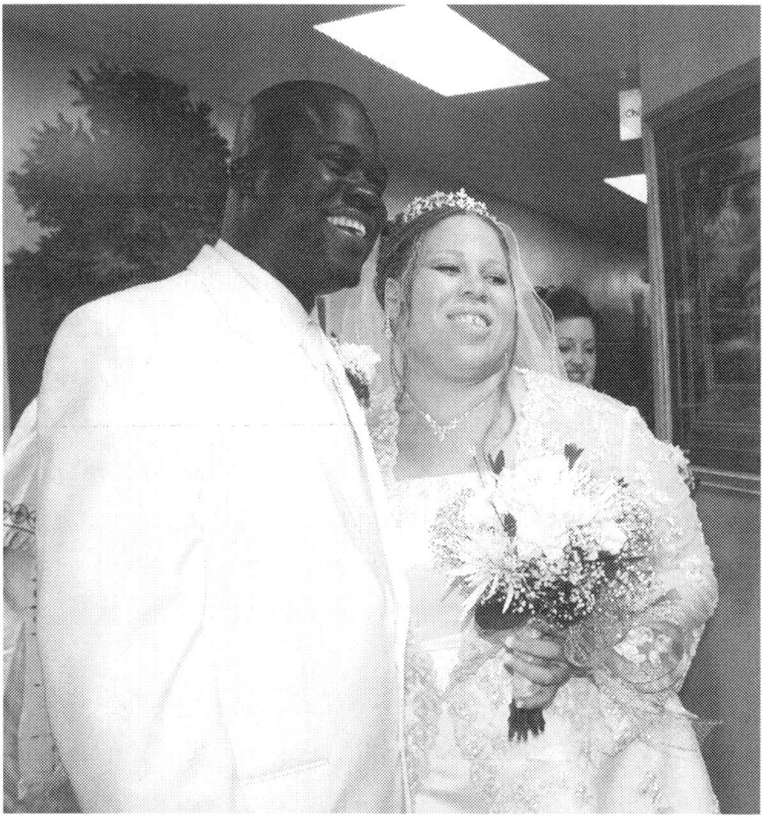

Suzy and Ansu's wedding

21

The Future

Suzy and Ansu moved in with their relative Mosiray and his family. She returned to her job as a home health aide, but Ansu was unable to get documents that would allow him to work until another year passed. He was learning American culture but felt like he wasn't doing anything useful. Finally the necessary authorization came and he found employment in a nursing home kitchen. Times were hard; Suzy and Ansu walked everywhere or took the train or bus. Finally they were able to save enough for a car and later their own apartment.

One day Suzy suggested, "You should go to school." Ansu became confused about this considering their bills and responsibilities. Suzy encouraged him: "Let's just try. Further education will allow you to do great things both here and in Africa." Ansu is interested in public health and would like to work for the U.N. The first step was enrolling in prerequisite nursing courses at Delaware County Community College. He also found a better job as a caregiver for mentally challenged men, going to school during the day and working at night. Suzy and Ansu both graduated from a certified nursing assistant course, and Ansu has continued his studies. He expects to receive his associate's degree in nursing in 2014.

The couple talked of starting their family after Ansu's graduation. One day he picked up a pregnancy test kit for future use. He didn't mention it to Suzy, but she found it and decided to try it out. The test seemed to read a positive result, but Suzy assumed that her poor eyesight was causing her to interpret it incorrectly. She wasn't feeling any different than usual and was pretty sure she wasn't pregnant. Ansu wanted to make sure, and to their great surprise, lab work showed that she was eight weeks along in her pregnancy. They could hardly believe it and didn't share the news with anyone because it seemed so unreal. In fact, it didn't sink in until they finally saw their baby's image by ultrasound. Finally they became excited about the coming of a new family member.

A big problem was their lack of insurance, considering the high cost of giving birth. Suzy contacted various companies, and the response was always the same: "Are you already pregnant? Then we can't insure you." When she shared this news with her dad, Joe indignantly declared, "That can't be possible! There must be a way to get costs reduced!" He called Suzy's doctor's office and heard the same reply from a receptionist. Then he insisted, "There must be some alternative!" After a moment's hesitation, she gave the phone number of a medical clinic in Chester, Pennsylvania. “The cost is reasonable if you pay in advance,” she said. This was the answer they needed.

Ansu and Suzy’s baby boy was due in March, and we made plans to be there for the happy event if at all possible. Finally, Ansu called to say that Suzy was in the hospital and would soon be induced if the baby didn’t come naturally. He could not get off work, but Suzy’s cousin Fatu stayed with her at the hospital. Fatu also cooked food for us during our long day of waiting after the thirteen-hour trip from Indiana. Finally a C-section was deemed necessary. It was a difficult delivery, but we were all excited to welcome baby Joseph Humaru Kamara (named after his two grandfathers) on the evening of March 4, 2013. When Suzy commented that he looked just like Ansu except for his light-colored skin, Ansu laughed. “Just wait,” he said. “That will change!” His skin is perfect, beautiful ebony.

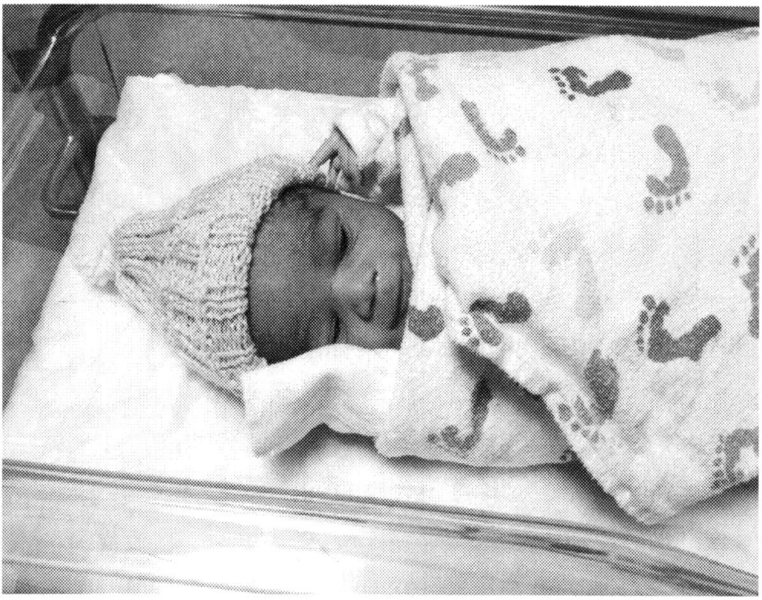

Baby Joseph

During her pregnancy, Suzy had worried that she would somehow pass on her insecure feelings about albinism to her baby boy. People might make negative comments to him about his "white" mother or voice inquisitiveness about differing skin tones in the family. Maybe Ansu would feel strange with her and the baby in public, although he had never expressed this in any way. She is surprised and pleased that there has been no negative feedback from anyone. Instead people stop her to exclaim, "Your baby is so beautiful!" These grandparents totally agree!

When Joseph was two weeks old, he and Suzy returned with us to Indiana until the end of June. It was wonderful for us, but Ansu was lonely without his wife and their new son. Back in Philadelphia her days caring for Joseph and their small apartment were long while Ansu attended school and joined study groups to assure good grades. He is not happy with less than A's! The weekends proved especially hard as his job with a mentally challenged client lasted from Friday afternoon through late Sunday evening. Suzy's astigmatism has not allowed her to drive, and so she and Joseph couldn't attend church or go anywhere else. Yet she believes God used this difficult time to teach her new lessons. She said,

> When Ansu first came to America and I was working as a home health aide, I was intrigued by a Hispanic man speaking on the radio. I usually didn't like to listen

to preachers, especially over radio or TV. For me church was a social event, the right thing to do. Yet I was enjoying hearing this man's accent and his message. He said that Jesus loves us and accepts us just as we are. He was reading Scripture and talking in layman's terms, and so I continued to listen.

Five years later, when Joseph and I were at home with no chance to go to church, I remembered that preacher. I thought his name was Raul, and when I googled it, I found him to be the pastor of a church in California. His sermons were online, and I began listening to them every morning. He was teaching through the Bible verse by verse, but he emphasized that God's message is always the same: "God loves you. Come to Him as you are."

He spoke of Jesus' death on the cross so that we could find salvation from our sin and its consequences. He also said that Jesus is coming back for those who believe in Him. We need to be ready. I knew this; I had often heard it during my childhood, but somehow it seemed more real to me now. I believe that God wanted me to go through those lonely days to take away all distractions so I could hear Him speak to me.

I began to see things differently, realizing that as a Christian I am in a battle, but "our struggle is not against flesh and blood" as the Bible says (Eph. 6:12). People may be against me, but the real battle is with our enemy, the devil. God wants me to love people as He loves them. He wants to give me a passion for reaching people with the message of God's love and forgiveness.

I had forgotten about the Bible my friend Heather Earnest had given me. I happened to find it again and read her inscription in the front: "January 9, 2000. On the surface God's power is not always visible, but the person with faith knows God is behind it all." I did believe that God was "behind it all." He has known me all along and has been working out his purposes in my life. I recommitted my life to Him.

Many years after Suzy wrote her poem, "The Truth about Me," her dream has come true. She had written:

Well, until that day comes, and these feelings run out
Of this heart filled with pain and this doubt,
I'll just say a prayer and endure this time

Until my beauty has come and good feelings unwind.

Suzanne is now able to thank God for the way He created her and for all He has done in her life, including bringing her a special husband and baby son. She has given her life to serving Him in the way He plans. She finally (and rightly) believes she is His beautiful and much-loved child, no longer a "little lost angel." God is leading and the future is bright.

Ansu, Suzy, and Joseph Humaru Kamara

Afterword

Dear Reader:

Thank you for joining me on this journey through Suzanne's story. Perhaps you have been mystified by some of the statements in this book. Maybe you wonder about the meaning of "giving" or "recommitting our lives to God" or "knowing God's leading for our lives."

At the time I was learning Psalm 34:7: "Delight yourself in the LORD, and He will give you the desires of your heart," I heard that I could have a personal relationship with God through His Son Jesus. I learned that He loves me, and it was suggested that I put my own name in this verse of Scripture: "For God so loved Pat, that He gave His only begotten Son, that if Pat would believe in Him, she should not perish, but have eternal life" (John 3:16 paraphrased).

Then I read that He is knocking at my heart's door, so to speak: "Behold, I stand at the door and knock; if anyone [I could put in my own name again] hears My voice and opens the door, I will come in to him and will dine with him, and he with Me" (Revelation 3:20).

Another Scripture states, "The thief comes only to steal and kill and destroy; I came that they may have life, and have it abundantly. I am the good shepherd; the good shepherd lays down His life for the sheep" (John 10:10–11).

These gracious words describe Jesus, the Good Shepherd, who *did* lay down His life for us, His sheep, when He died on a Roman cross.

You see, by God's standard we can never measure up. We can never be as holy and perfect as He is. But Jesus died so that we could be forgiven our wrongdoing and made clean before God's holiness (1 John 1:9, paraphrased).

At the tender age of nineteen, I wanted that relationship with a loving Savior, who would also represent me before the Father, God. Like any relationship, it takes time and effort to build, time to learn what He is like through His Word, the Bible, and time talking with Him in prayer, time getting to know Him. I started on a journey with Him by opening up my heart and asking Him to please come in to be my Savior, my Good Shepherd, and my guide through life. I believe *Unexpected Destiny* attests to His faithfulness.

Now I am suggesting and praying that you, dear reader, will open your heart to begin a journey with the One who provides life in abundance. He likely has unexpected things in store for you as well. Seek a relationship with Jesus. Try Him. You will not regret it.

In His Name,
Pat

About the Author

Pat Estes, a retired teacher with writing and editing experience, lives in Indianapolis. She and her husband worked as missionaries in Sierra Leone, West Africa, for nine years. They are blessed with two adopted children from diverse cultural backgrounds, along with their spouses and three grandchildren.

Notes

1. Deeanne Gist, *Courting Trouble*, three novels in one volume, novel 3: *The Trouble with Brides* (Minneapolis, MN: Bethany, 2007), 190–191.
2. Hank Paulson with Don Richardson, *Beyond the Wall* (Ventura, CA: Regal, 1982), 24–25.
3. Janet Field Heath, *Little Lost Angel* (Chicago: Rand McNally, 1953).
4. Catherine Marshall, *To Live Again* (New York: McGraw Hill, 1957), 334.
5. Ray Boltz (words and music), "Thank You," AA© copyright 1988, Gaither Music Co.